The Square Root of Beirut

OMAR SABBAGH

Published by Cinnamon Press
Meirion House
Glan yr afon
Tanygrisiau
Blaenau Ffestiniog
Gwynedd
LL41 3SU
www.cinnamonpress.com

The right of Omar Sabbagh to be identified as author of this work has been asserted by him in accordance with the Copyright, Designs and Patent Act, 1988. Copyright © 2011 Omar Sabbagh.
ISBN: 978-1-907090-54-7
British Library Cataloguing in Publication Data. A CIP record for this book can be obtained from the British Library.
All rights reserved. No part of this publication may be reproduced, stored in a retrieval system, or transmitted in any form or by any means, electronic, mechanical, photocopying, recording or otherwise without the prior written permission of the publishers. This book may not be lent, hired out, resold or otherwise disposed of by way of trade in any form of binding or cover other than that in which it is published, without the prior consent of the publishers.

Designed and typeset in Palatino by Cinnamon Press.
Cover from original artwork © Byblos (Jbeil) in Beirut by Michalakis Ppalis, agency: Dreamstime.com
Cover design by Jan Fortune
Printed in Poland

Cinnamon Press is represented in the UK by Inpress Ltd www.inpressbooks.co.uk and in Wales by the Welsh Books Council www.cllc.org.uk.

The publisher acknowledges support from Arts Council England Grants for the Arts

LOTTERY FUNDED

Acknowledgements

Some of these poems have previously appeared in the following: *Agenda, Agenda Online Broadsheets, Banipal, Envoi, Kenyon Review Online, Poetry Review, Poetry Wales, The Reader, Stand, The Warwick Review.*

The quote from *Sexus* by Henry Miller is used with kind permission of Harper Collins.

The quote from Theodor W. Adorno's, 'Refuge for the homeless', in *Minima Moralia* is used with kind permission of Verso.

The author would like to thank Dr Jan Fortune and Dr Fiona Sampson for their encouragement and support, editorial and otherwise, in what were and are troubled times.

Contents

Epistle Home	9
The War Abroad And Within	10
Legitimacy Crisis	11
Slim Reportage From Beirut	12
Nub And Rub In Beirut	13
Bearing Witness	14
A Land Starved Of Caritas	15
Perspective From The AUB Gardens	16
One-Way Streets	17
Arachne In Beirut	18
Achilles' Decade	19
The Square Root Of Beirut	20
4th May, 1981	21
Still In The House Of My Father	22
On Lebanon	23
As the night is a colony that will not wait	24
Prodigy	26
Sublimation	28
Heart On Stone	29
Thrown From The Real	30
Less Than A Thought Away	31
A Rival To Incontinence	32
The Kindness Of The Man	33
At The Burial	34
A Day On	35
Poetry	36
My House	37

Quatrains After Maud	38
First Bone	39
At-One-Ment	40
Apology Over Shattered China	41
A Window	42
The Streets Shouting 'It's Not Your Poem', And Other Circus Acts	44
Berry-Alive	45
Augustine Becomes Dependent	46
Beginning With The Rigging	47
Mediation	48
As Opposed To The Ellipses Of The Blind	49
A 'Social' Winter	50
Holier Than Thou	51
A Deconstruction Of Suffering And The Confessional	52
Sonnet Of The (Latent) Stalker	53
On Loneliness	54
Reel	56
To An Amateur Doctor	57
His Confessor	58
In The Beginning	59
Ligaments Between The Notes	60
On Anger	61
The Hiding Place	62
Empty, Emptying	63
The Solitary, His Fate In Dream	64

'When one is trying to do something beyond his known powers it is useless to seek the approval of friends. Friends are at their best in moments of defeat -- at least that is my experience. Then they either fail you utterly or they surpass themselves. Sorrow is the great link -- sorrow and misfortune. But when you are testing your powers, when you are trying to do something new, the best friend is apt to prove a traitor. The very way he wishes you luck, when you broach your chimerical ideas, is enough to dishearten you. He believes in you only in so far as he knows you; the possibility that you are greater than you seem is disturbing, for friendship is founded on mutuality...'

Henry Miller, *Sexus*

'The general fact is simple. Poetry is sane because it floats easily in an infinite sea; reason seeks to cross the infinite sea, and so make it finite. The result is mental exhaustion.... To accept everything is an exercise, to understand everything is a strain. The poet only desires exaltation and expansion, a world to stretch himself in. The poet only asks to get his head into the heavens. It is the logician who seeks to get the heavens into his head. And it is his head that splits.'

G.K. Chesterton, *Orthodoxy*

The Square Root of Beirut

Sabiha and Bisher Faris, i.m.

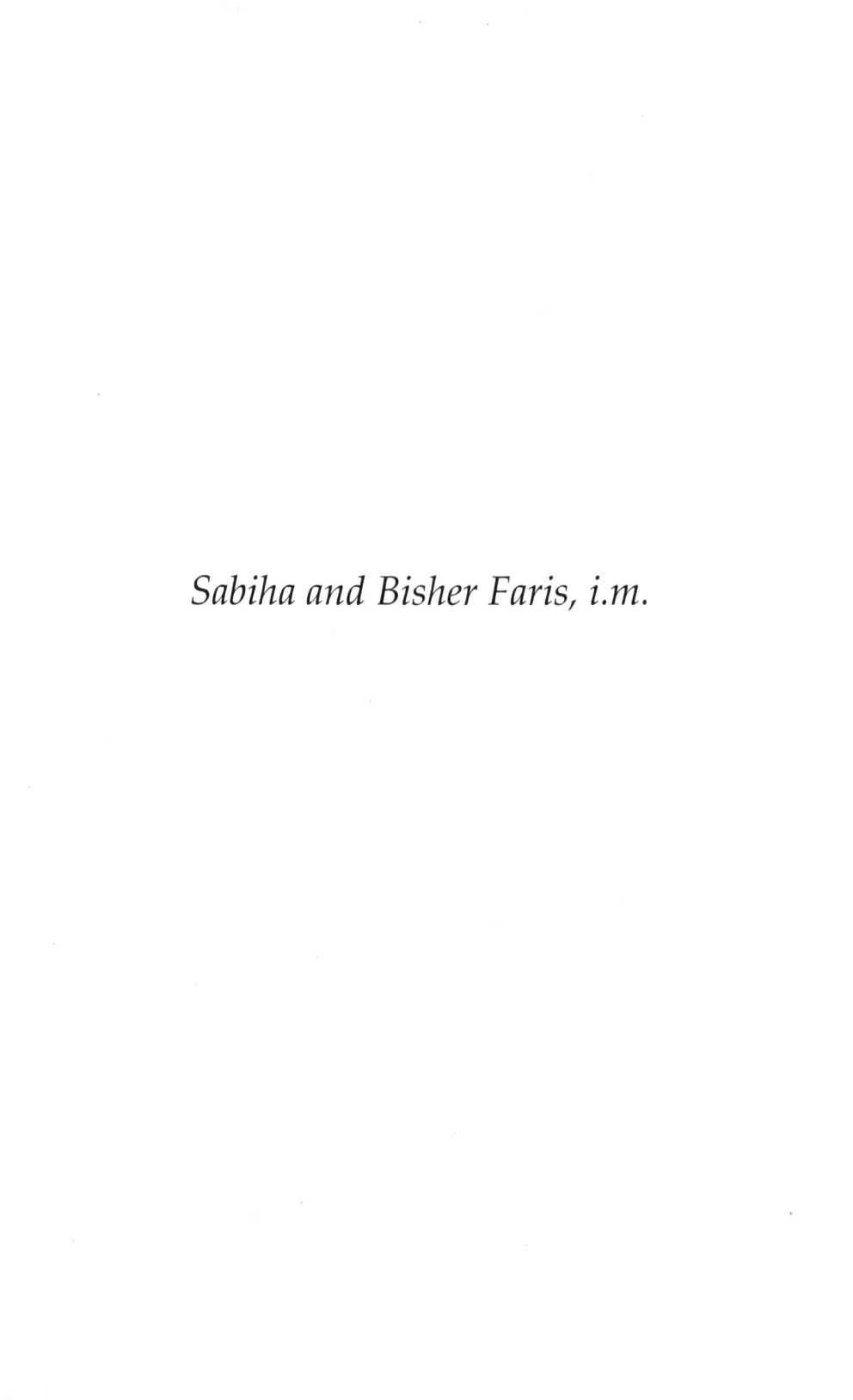

Epistle Home

I miss the chalk of my home
And the clay-red.
Knotting the tropes of a sudden nation
The poets here are maroon
As their rust-hued country.

The skyline, low and close,
Is too heat-heavy to trust.
And the average man's a mote.
I watch my parents grow smaller here,
Slowly shrivel, as with age,

But with added impetus.
The mind goes as the body's crossed
Out. The mind loses itself in the mind's moss
Of multiple motives
Among the littler heroes.

The War Abroad And Within

In spite of being born during my parents' exile

Born amidst roughage, most sad,
Your first grudge was with the wax
You were made of. There were sacks
Of sleep behind you, or at least
Of the edge of sleep, its winking precipice.

Eight months in the womb and
Barely a smile where everything was
Round and everything mixed and danced.
The fresh air was first to drive a knife,
Before the doctor snipped then sewed

Your belly. Everyone was cheery and spoke of
Mown lawns along whose borders you'd grow
As lush and as steady, awaiting what might blossom.
They spoke of dawn at mid-morning and
Brushed your wet hair. You were born

To look forward to that spark they recalled
Amid mist and confusion and dead warriors.
You were the second layer of the palimpsest
They'd made of war. Illusions remained, however,
And so did the snicker of ghosts.

Legitimacy Crisis

Starbucks, Verdun, Beirut

It's still and quiet on Sundays here,
but there are no gardens
to wrap and be wrapped.

The only thing to stare at here
is an ashen floor
and the fire of the afternoon,

a cooled gun-metal sky.
Silence bides by her claims
mid-sip in the café…

Men walk by, for the first time
filling their slippers,
daring poets to full rhyme,

the kitsch number,
as if home were home for once…
It's still and quiet on Sundays here

amid slave-galleons,
amid hidden
gallons of tears.

The stick and stone and the edgy fear
rive and rive and rive here,
still a nation in its teenage years.

Slim Reportage From Beirut

Café Younes, Hamra, Beirut

It remains a question of scaffolding,
Curlicues clocking the unfolding
To a sharp ear. Claws hatchets on claws,
Political commentators dream
Cheaply across the table: angry oral wishes.

A nation of roasting shopkeepers,
Roasting in their shrinking world,
Are odds and ends between the posters –
Thereby seeking only a figment of order,
Wave upon wave of curling water:

And the steam's the thing!
Valves in a city of valves…
Meanwhile, the youth continues to halve
Halves, counting time in frustration,
Awaiting swift chance to rise

Like some proverb's phoenix on
The sweaty, burly shoulders
Of a more vulgar kind of Mammon.
As for me, I continue to gambol
Amidst roulette balls and faulty spins:

A dawn stag with the steady reputation
Of finery and fighting horns…
Imagine the nation as a hand:
It's all digits, there is no palm.
It's all digits, there is no calm.

Nub And Rub In Beirut

Starbucks, Verdun, Beirut

Gauge the loss, the offering
of slit hands in handshakes,
the desperado's clinch.

Later in the day they'll
stumble upwards to rococo flats,
deluxe takes on home and hearth

but for where the children play,
slinging their joy like
outriders and skirmishers

deployed,
a leavened leeway far away –
strands, islands.

God is eaten without the mouth,
without the tongue,
without the lips,

no part of waxy bodies slipped
into straitjackets.
God is loved by way of the lice –

soothsayers revered by
these jailed, highly strung
minds replaced by seam-thin zips and wigs.

Bearing Witness

The youth, Café Younes, Hamra, Beirut

As wonder lost its genital verve,
The stream spoke to the rocks
And briefly curbed its flow:

Was I ever so young
Or so close to you, my navel,
So ready to be hit to tears
And plundered, hoodwinked
By such tender years
The wool of the ewe's yet to know?

The rock spoke in a low voice.
Said many things, and many things twice.
The water listened
And pleated itself, slowed
So nothing would be missed.

Fold after fold of clear water
Turned drapery like the rocks,
They conversed
And so they still converse.

A Land Starved Of Caritas

Janus-faced, a rabble at work and play.
There are no witnesses to say which way
Their stark Caesar went, their evanescent
Leader dolling out the black and the white.

Legends without a mind to guide them
Hold sway. The people are starving at the seams,
From which ill-fed, grim-faced monsters
Riot, feeding on the grey of the poisoned air.

The land is a land of metal, cold to the touch.
The land is a land of clouds, from which
Meaning is sieved, as at the end of a smoking gun.
At the pierced midriff, chaos spills and runs

Instead of crystal-clear, cool water.
Lebanon is not found where I sought her,
On a hip-shaped hill of chunky Cedars.
Her breasts are dry and scrawny, wilted members.

Perspective From The AUB Gardens

For Walid Semaan

The aerials are taut
and have petals like roses
and are stood labias
like roses.

Between root and root
both the garden
and the travelling youth
choose
and are chosen:

a green,
a green libertinage.

There are no walls, no bars.
Each walkway winds into all
and birds soaring are
and cohere
as ciphers conferred.

In the distance, a plain, unadorned
music is heard;
it intones and intends
the rustling of small wings
in the umbrage.

Something, as yet misunderstood,
is born.
        Something small and good,
but for the pinched skin
and the squeaking
of the neighbourhood.

One-Way Streets

You wake in the morning with burly wishes
After your dreams, walking a plank or seam

And leaping outwards into the abyss
Of day's splayed light, neat remit, remittance.

Then the dead flower of the night
Comes to life as a waking nightmare.

The trees in this land produce martyrs
And suicides, the willing and the unwilling.

Each street sign pacing your hooded journey
Reads like the entrance to a mole's abode.

Denizens here offer their love
Only amidst the undergrowth.

You'll leave this land where choice begins
By a mint and purple sea.

By the Corniche it ripples with white
And buoys a voice.

Arachne In Beirut

The nation is a child at the window of its childhood.
In strange skins and in tints on the wall
Monsters lie and ripple,
                wave after wave.
Fear is no longer a moment's portion. Bathed,
Baptized in murk,
           dollops, confusion,
                        a story of hay
And needles.

There is pity, only a few boats at sea.
There are whole tables of lack, lunching
With leers that trap and are trapped.
Webs echo outwards, slim and sticky
From Arab hands, Arab fingers.
This is their staple.

Where is quiddity, that spider
Where all walk on eight legs?

Achilles' Decade

The first time we judge, says the philosopher,
Is the first time we feel disgust.
From then on the copula's predatory lust's
A moment we were prey, tossed, premature,
Gestalt-less
To our hollow, innermost core.

I have burrowed too long, O caring care…

Where exactly does the body enter Mind?
At the heel, says the myth,
Where flesh and widening bone are kissed
In a bloody embrace,
A magic laying-on of hands.

In a watery world, a kind of Lethe, then,
I lived pure among the fish, a king of men.

This past decade though, on wincing land, so
Slimly pierced and forced to grow
That I no longer know – O
Caring care –
Who or how or why to forgive

Or love
Anymore.

The Square Root Of Beirut

On the stone wall, shapes and a script.
Drunken hands have lived in wet colour
That's turned to desiccate mud here
On the stone wall. Sift

For words amidst the dirt.
Presently, yes presently they'll emerge
From this echolalia of hurt, split, forked
Tongues layering the concrete streets

As split echoes echo from traipsing bodies.
And the salty scent of the sea's no remedy.
There are no remedies. Alpha and Omega split here
Into a Manichee heaven and a Manichee hell.

4th May, 1981

And now, a warm draught across my eyes' beam,
A sort of confusion and dithering, a dream-idiom.
The only thing I can see comes swiftly in delirium:
A hot sweltering, its sense: the belly of what solely seems…

And then, with full intent, I think back to my
Mother's love, when I was calmly tenanted by
Miles of fierce affection, and a deletion of style
And stylization, when pain stood in line, packed, filed.

And with more intent than that, like the Will behind
And above the Word, I saw my father so clear and crystalline,
Then put one and one together, built the ultimate rhyme,
Saw my birth, the bloody burst, wailing, life's ruddy sign.

The nurse, I'm told, descried my beauty through maroon;
But failed to see the fateful berth of Narcissus: his doom.

Still In The House Of My Father

Watch where they leap, *sea-sprinters!*
And the sunny air as their blessed hinge…

Dolphins, grey and blue and innocent,
Their long noses especially meant
To scent where the wine-dark sea bends
To the low-lying, murky corridors
Of the black-backed, white-bellied sharks…

And what if I were to run, tandem with the sea,
Tandem with the moon –
Would I know where the bane lurks,
Where the boon?

Would I be one of the telling questions?
The ones that get the water to give up its salt?
The ones, by the shore, the crabs' claws seem to pray for,
Twisted as they are, crawling jagged as they are?

My sight reaches that far
Only in the house of my father,

Guided by a simple, licit star
And a sprawling awry cursive
Of hurt and crimson letters.

On Lebanon

For Fouad Sanyoura

The two pins at either end
Of the arc of this story are thorns
And my poetry speaks to where I was born.

I want to blend madness with madness here,
To walk straight with two bent shoulders
And a rickety spine that shrieks like a cricket
At dawn...
                    My homeland's a storm
In me, a deep decision made
Between shoulder-blade and shoulder-blade.

As the night is a colony that will not wait

For my parents, Mohamad and Maha Sabbagh

As the night is a colony that will not wait
And all the daylight-days' foreboding is
A tune played belatedly, double-crossed
On the instrument of the mind,
I write this urgent message line by line.

Mother of my will, father of my thoughts –

As I turn this corner metaphysical,
Call all my yesterdays forgiven at a glance,
Say two and two is now fork and knife,
Not the four-square rigid stance
Of number, drilled number –

And for all your lies, after all the years
You've treated me, medically, O so medically!
With those parentally-sweet, singed
And *doucely*-tinged pliers,

Where I was a twisted screw in the minuet,
In the wooden battlement
Of family –

Mother of my will,
Father of my thoughts, you'll
Be the platitude gimme's once again,
The inversely-proportioned
Begetters of the bill
I owe, owing less, growing happier
As I turn with age.

In my current heart there is an acorn:
Let it strap on its burden of green-fringed light
And become the upward avenue for
A wetted mouth, tongue a slipstream,
Words spread out to all in all like
The moon's baby white.

Prodigy

Start with a comma, so they know
I was there before I was born –
that the womb was only an alibi.

Tell them that in childhood I realized
that only the lucky are given
a little authorship in life, a pittance.

I knew, you see, so very quickly,
that just as the grown-ups would steer
what we saw, what we heard, and what

we endeavoured – I knew that even later
in life, things would be the same.
I was small, I was short, but I divined

the ubiquity of bullying. Fate,
and even character, were things of which
I knew nothing. I could not moralise.

But I knew that we, as a species, were not safe.
What can I say? I suppose I had psychic gifts,
that I was forward in the mind. It's eighteen years

since I was eight. And when they write
my biography, whenever, however
long it takes, I know that I will still be

one of you, one of us, a puppet
steered by all the things I love,
all the things I hate, and the something in me,

spinning fractional within,
that sees the map, sees the X penciled in,
but also sees

the pirate chuckling with the pen.

Sublimation

Eagle is munching mouse again,
                                              and I can feel
the way the meat will flow from the bone of its nose
swiftly on to summer, big muscle of the sky.

Heart On Stone

My father says his heart is on me and that my
Heart is on the stone.
The Arabic proverb invades on poetry
But is a weak reply to pain.

The stone, father, is in both our hearts,
What lets them, like solid brick-like pips,
Knock against each other in the wind,
What makes that clacking sound
Each time we argue
Like terriers without the defence of ribs.

Thrown From The Real

Was it hard, to lie like that, on a bed of prickly pines?
To be always the remainder of someone else's discourse,
That need of yours the world's desire can never reach?

In your infancy of short leaping legs
You were one with that desire
Because that desire was one with you –

You'd a mother like a hall of pillows
And the beard of your father was a law
That bristled soft to the touch.

Now the harrow hits you hard, un-begotten adulthood.
You were never ready for the hurry and the harry
Of the market place, where you're supposed to trade goods.

You weren't informed what a numb finger it could be.
Too used to a supple muscle dressed as an artistry,
You weren't ready for the bludgeoning noise

Of digging machines – it came as such a surprise!
So you take it easy, continue as a lily on a lake,
And summarily account all from infancy a waste and a fake.

Less Than A Thought Away

For Mohamad Sabbagh

For all the virtue of the just and every work that is wrought by the virtue of the just is nothing but this, that the Son is begotten of the Father.
Meister Eckhart

When I think of what I owe you
I think of a thing less than a thought away,
Something with the speed of a sting
Or prayer, both being closer than blood to skin.

I see tears in your eyes that you move to wipe
After the moving motive weapon-work
Of the Hollywood movie
That so reminds you of me…

Yes, I suppose I've been typical at times,
With the wan smile of the madman
Looking for rhymes, patterns, lines
Of coalescence… the mind's tumescence!

And I'm glad you were there to teach me the lessons
In real time, a pound of my pain to a pound
Of yours. Less and less do I listen for the sounds
Of hammers and tongs, of punishment and

The absent heart of the world.
You are pip to my fruit, father,
Socket and keystone: warmer, warmer,
In the cold, low-travelled travails

Of a chilled decade
That started with a girl…
Less than a thought away,
Skin of my skin, still.

A Rival To Incontinence

For Sabiha Faris, i.m.

Do you remember how we walked between the hedgerows
in the park, I at four aching to grow, you
aching at my aching? A grandmother walked past us
hobbling on her stick, her other arm wrapped helplessly round
her daughter. She was thin as a wick, thin
as the air billowing the wick, close, close to the ground.

You turned to me and asked me if, when
in your low-bound, groundbreaking senility,
I would be the bundle of tender muscles
for you to lumber upon till the time came for you to see
the dead as equals. I ran to pluck you a pale blue
flower, symbol of the sky you were to me.

The Kindness Of The Man

For Bisher Faris, i.m.

Imagine a home with too many rooms –

That's how his kindness is remembered
As the black river receives him…

How many deaths there are in one death!
How much power in all
The sudden, sharp-angled oaths
Of others: as ever,
Hindsight building its sturdy wailing wall.

I turn to my mother, whose keening wail
For her brother's
A thousand throats' misery,

A thousand white sails
Hatched from somewhere beyond the horizon,
Impossibly – God's fleet,
God's white woe, God's mourning livery.

At The Burial

Bisher Faris, R.I.P.

I would the great world grew like thee,
Who grewest not alone in power
And knowledge, but by year and hour
In reverence and in charity.
                    Alfred, Lord Tennyson, CXIV, *In Memoriam*

Water in my eyes matches water in my body
As the dead man becomes his fullest self
Swaddled by the earth –
The lowering movement a new kind of poverty
In which to lie, a vanishing of itself.

We are all metal warriors now,
Slowly smelted by the sun…

We are all feathers now
Blown to naked stems, like thistledown,
Limbless but un-shriven…

What's given in the cozen of family's
Now given…

            Which way survival
Amidst the silly gale of grief
And the feeling of a lightning that pinpoints a leaf?

The man is dead, incredible as it is,
And tears are wasted on the blessed.

A Day On

For Bisher Faris, i.m.

A day spent, sifted since his death,
And we gravitate with our sour thoughts,
The bitter air around us stressed
With uncanny births, fantasy's children.

Summer's no slack vacancy for love.
All, as I'd expect, are witlessly busy
And march forward, file after file, numb,
And end where we, bereft of a sudden,

Have just begun.
Does the death of a loved one
Deepen the grooves,
The sallow rills of the mind moved

To render blood into insight?
It's at times like these I heed
The emotions of the blind,
The long-wrought wreckage

Of the deaf and dumb –
All who live under the one-time sign
Of catastrophe
And a limit-language of agony;

All who dwell in a church of pain –
Its spineless liturgy
Without remission –
Marking in the margins

Of some tome known only to them
Death's cursive, Death's dance,
Its grim ballet of breaking waves,
Its slyly awful game with chance.

Poetry

For Maha Evers

I wanted to write about revolution
like a love story where everyone
in the world had glanced
at everyone else, at least once –
where we'd all seen through each other
and the earth had really circled
white to the bone,
                     and then
real passion could begin
and reign like a pregnant woman:
                           Revolution
as a new chaos of intimacy
too public for the revolutionaries,

where I could touch you in awe like a statue
that comes to life from the margin
of some unknown elsewhere
to kiss without the usual unfair
consequences.

Rhythm, and *le mot juste*
taking the plunge into us –
that's the love I want.

My House

In a time of hunters and gatherers,
When a brawny arm was as valid as a tooth,
I offered her my love

And waited for the surge in her olive
Eyes; but nothing could soothe
Her witch's icy, slicing anger.

She was cold on the ache of my heart,
Her tongue's wild accent skewing my art.

Let ice sleep with ice then,
Deaf ear with deaf ear,
Tongue shattered and scattered
In its native mouth…

These words comprise my brawn
And remain: square pillars of my house.

Quatrains After Maud

As wide, ragged and peacefully grim
As she is when, in a smile, she's with him,
Is the canyon, the beige and rocky womb,
Where, both lost and at a loss, they met: a sum.

Auburn and eyes lifted with prettiness,
She was a thing of hinges, a winking princess
Who was a lullaby behind the door
And what was reaped in secrecy, a secret lore.

And now, in the manners of the clock,
I hear a please and a thank you dock
In the harbor of my mind, a proper girl
And a convenient, wrapped more than a pearl.

She's anger and bilious rage in the manger.
She's the babe's hair-shirt instead of cloth.
She's the pain swaddling the dumb earth
Seen from the moon: hilly, white, without care.

First Bone

For C

Our feeling, dazzled, flutters like a flock of birds in the woman's radiance. And as birds seek refuge in the leafy recesses of a tree, feelings escape into the shaded wrinkles, the awkward movements and inconspicuous blemishes of the body we love, where they can lie low in safety. And no passerby would guess that it is just here, in what is defective and censurable, that the fleeting darts of adoration nestle.
                                                    Walter Benjamin, *One-Way Street*

Great ovals of bony white –
                              the knees I saw,
rapt, and with what was like
an ear's alertness, the ear's notorious
suspicion and passion –
                              your knees
    were ready to hatch.

And what sort of progeny
                              do you think, love,
would emerge, ripe to the touch?

It was the first time I'd lurch
                              and leer,
wholly riven
                by the sight of your flesh,
    flesh on bone,
                taut and fresh.

But you know it, love.
                          Fresh
from this happy dehiscence,
                          the bone
had a baby of bone.

At-One-Ment

I whisked her away like a sum total,
A beauty bloated
By years of comparison.

Nothing weighed less
And nothing was
So ready to be spilled
To the deep echoic call
Of slick night creatures.

Love, like a raging angel, fell

Into the pit of vapid years, and sped,
Like the light,
Into ever new editions, till,

On the edge's inch of dusk,
I found the true hue of her
That I could trust,

And we made a lavender love,
Each to each an awning,
Now oblivious like the concussed…

Apology Over Shattered China

And then your bickered face becomes a dam,
A high and shuttered stare; and your long blond hair –
The dicing flick, the lightning spin – gives cuts
And yellow burns: miffed and stifled woman...

As you leave now with poisoned eyes
And pursed lips like the slammed-down
Butt of a rifle, I think again of how
You giggled and giddily apostrophized,
Like I was your one and only lovely child,
That first time we stumbled to a kiss...

You caressed the hair above my temples
And mocked, approaching, softly shocked
But willing me on: *now take the chance*
You said, *now is the time to consume*
And maximize the spell of first things felt...

And the love that night was perfect,
Like sipping milk from a rock:
The rocky deliverance was coarse yet
More lovely for that: no buts. And so...

                                   It's *sorry*
Now for the way things always end
So drained, siphoned and flat. It's *sorry*
That shattered china never mends, and
Sorry, pure and cold as sail-white wind.

A Window

For Imogen Mary

I was thinking forward to the soft sandy thrills
Of a weekend of naked feet, naked at the beach.
She's coming to visit me out in Spain in a week –
This morning ten empty years were killed
From their decay; a rut, a ditch, a gap was filled.

This morning breakfast in bed never appeared;
But the woman to my right delivered her lips,
Fat pale red, into the arms of mine; our lids
Descended hard onto our noses, and we kissed:
Though breakfast in bed never appeared.

What a shock it is
To be and get rocked and mellifluous
As the word itself: *Romance*
Rolling off the upper bridge of our mouths,
Our tongues like joggers, panting for breath
But still going on, and farther north
Than the farthest reaches of the poles –

We stretch, we stretch the meaning of our lives
When we kiss. We are birds in a hive,
Somehow out of place, but somehow too
There to be made to feel comfortable,
If a little abducted with the buzz of things.

In a week's time's past a life of gloom
Has been emptied of its dead weight.
I met her listening to some reggae
In a reggae bar, thinking of all the doom molested spliffs
Had done me. This morning,

There was no breakfast in bed
But the two of us. Munching on the soft white bread
Of her shoulders, I thought back to some of the dead
Years gone by: would that time past could talk
For itself: it'd say, most probably, *I'm here to stay!*

But we know, in the learnt lessons of our love,
That the past is only past when it's passed
With someone close as light through glass.

The Streets Shouting 'It's Not Your Poem', And Other Circus Acts

Those lousy clowns

Streakers with knots painted on their chests,
How wonderful it is
To see the truly naked, the truly run, the truly down,
With three dimensions on their chests.
                               The streets are crying
Because they're empty. Everyone is flabbergasted and gone.
Only the circus has come to town. The bear tamer
And high wire act are drinking with the clowns.
The lions are loose, but cannot roar. Streakers
Too used to strictnesses. I've said it before:
                                         O Kaiser...

Berry-Alive

For Tariq Ali

If you bury me, you'll slit the slitful of berries,
I pray. Wouldn't want to be a live wire, worrying, worrying
For all those agonistic days like a stick in the mud.
They've meddled with me, my love. Their medal-love
Like no other (no *other*.) Bother and bore and bury, yes, bury,
Against a brother of the berries and other
                                                            such fruit.

Augustine Becomes Dependent

The drawn drapes of eternity
Allow us a sunlit look-see:
The risen smell
Of fresh gardenias, say; Spring
Sprung as a lifeline, a necklace
Of lemon and sensual cream.

But all this came late in the day,
A siesta. Tested and hunted
Like game, from dawn to morning,
Sainthood waited to be born
From all that raucous noise.
It was all a question of mastery,
A singer over a song.

Now music lifts me
From note to note, aporetic and
In the meld,
Like a sip of God,
Where I no longer grab and hold,
But am madly held.

Beginning With The Rigging

And this wingless mast
Stands ready
To be quilted against the sea,
A calm tan torso and chest
Awaiting the trigger of touch.

Mediation

I'll start with a question, then
Let it trail like a voice, an
Opened scar on the air,

Before I make a decision...

I'll put myself in a word's care,
Or a litany's, or a prayer's,

Or a grimy scrawl of language
Awakening between my lips,
A savage adage
As potent and heavy as a man
Wishing for a woman's hips...

I'll feel that ought implies can
And that I'll never drown
In the wake of what I come to understand
In the midst of grinding an
Hallowed medium,
In the midst of its most proper gale.

Poet: see him!
In the mirror that disavows your frown!
In the clink and clank of the jail
Of your most intimate throat and sound,

The silver prison
Where pain begins
To sliver
And ends

As a trace remembered,
A golden facet of air,
An eye, an ear
Opening inwards.

As Opposed To The Ellipses Of The Blind

Not that this present
Meeting of eyes is so bitter,
But that without distance
And an effort at forgetting
The foul-smelling weeds in between,
You'll find neither spirit nor letter
Of what has been, as forestry, as unsurpassable bloom.

Reach back into the pit of memory and exhume
The fossil of yourself as yet unexposed.
Holding it safe between two hands,
Alighting on it
With the menace of too much sight,
Put it on the mantelpiece and let it
Feed the various ellipses of the blind.

This is you, remember, un-harried.
This is you among the sweeter meats,
The hapless hurry of a child as yet
Unaware that sentences might be
Sentences.
Walk with yourself and learn,
Even if the bouncing ball is your poem.

A 'Social' Winter

For Ali Zaraket

It was turning into a social winter
And all I could do was make a bowl
From my palms, a dome's cupola
Upturned;
      there was no lit grace, solace
Or warmed-up succor. No door ajar,
No window's narrative

And no rude tale told from sill to sill,
Echoic and riotous as childhood.
Even ellipses were deemed hale, good –

A nation's looser djinns, her crass *agon*.

And *pathos*? Mere letters in a kettle –

Words, worlds
On the edge of steam and infinite loss.

Holier Than Thou

Wrong life cannot be lived rightly.
        Theodor W. Adorno, 'Refuge for the homeless', in *Minima Moralia*

No, I am like that dove! Nothing more is felt
Than that. Zero else, and to the elses, and other
Heroisms. A Sultan of words like him, an offense
Against your insults and surds. Don't take offence, but
And other butts. You are (and were) the whole problem.

A Deconstruction Of Suffering And The Confessional

There is a boy screaming outside.
A pair of cutlets, his lungs seem to shrink as they're singed.
His cry reaches me, here, on the inside

And I wonder who he is,
Wonder what his knickknacks of suffering are,
What hobbyhorse of pain carries him so far

From home. And I can tell he's far from home
Because the tone of his voice is foreign,
Not only to me, but to him as well – a doubled heathen

In a country of rich and thinly civilized folk.
At the tip of agony, his wailing shriek,
The walls of my flat begin to shimmer, equivocate,

As if what were here were there.
Outside becomes inside: we meet in the middle
As one, and he confides in me this riddle:

Whatever's blue with shame's on a bloodless track,
Whatever's in defence will soon attack:
Look for me: I'm the fifth vertebra you cannot see –

Even the mirror hides me. Here,
Where you and I meet, midland and invisible, nothing's chosen,
You know who you are and in an instant I am broken.

Sonnet Of The (Latent) Stalker

For C

There was a jacket for it.
What she managed to say had borders,
Borders for the bombs she lit
And then watched explode over her shoulder.

It was a fog-bedraggled night,
A night more fit for dinosaurs or
Numinous unicorns, holders
Of the human fiction kit –

Much like the future:
A writ without a writ.
Splayed across that steep blue precipice
I was a knight. And no round kiss,

However succulent,
Could make my wrists desist.

On Loneliness

Each night,
a bomb and a tomb.
Of all the dead each night,

one still alive is plucked out and led
to a special room
in the house of the dead.

Once there, he can only mime
the ending procedures,
spreading his arms and legs,

dancing his drama along the seams
of the underworld,
amongst those now beyond time

and the expressive pearl
of his body-language.
What exactly he's doing there,

still alive enough to feel out of place,
he doesn't know. Death's infamous
brittle face

is everywhere, continued by mirrors,
bone-clean and sparse amidst
the smells of putrid outgrown flesh.

Enough time passes and this one
alive in death's bleak kingdom
grows beyond the sum

of a natural life,
so wonders why
his skin still wraps his heart so

well, why love still grows
inside of him, one notch above hope,
and how those he left behind have coped

without him.

Meanwhile, the dead still pile past him
in columns and rows, him still wondering
what sin it was that has him still

in its claws, talons, paws,
still hampered from reentering
at life's green door.

Each night
he feels more alone,
clad in white like the unborn.

Each night,
a ripping red blazonry
mars his way back home.

Reel

For Adam Phillips

An interpretation of bliss was what was missing
From the heurism of your kiss, that working idea
And hypothesis. We made love as large as fear
And for a while it was as if God was sitting
In the corner of the room, knitting our future.

Years ago, love, the wise men said there was no cure
For what I had, a madness sewn and matured
By millions of people and other lemmings and surds.
They spoke of the plethora of variables
That were in the mix of what was mental
In me, what was born and borne as catastrophe.

But I know better. The tropes know better.
Poetry is a hammer that breaks such fetters
Of spiel, is the jugular of what I feel
And what I will to leave as my life's lasting reel.

To An Amateur Doctor

After Leni in the bedroom, or, for Lina K.

A simple hop away, nubile in its dream-closeness:
Might I suggest – tossed in the warm swelter of your trust –
A different verse, Word, worldly tactic with which to emboss
This drained body, this supine, this rent, this split, distended lot
I come to inherit, a millionaire: but for the prompt place of the dot!

And if, as neighbor, you find the amity begins to rut and rot,
Disabled by too stark-white a light, truths too swift afoot,
Too taut a real in the glut and guts of my poems' moot
Dock in posterity – able amblers, feet in the cranny, feet
In the nook – if that's so and so, such and thus, let's not meet

Under the brass-conquered air, the trumpeters' sweet
And deep-lunged finale, their over-manly tweet-tweet…

Truth holed: if I'm an arrow, I'm my only bull's-eye.
I like being alone – slipshod – and am readied for its fires.

His Confessor

After Thomas Mann's Dr Faustus

When he was taut, slow, serious, he was trudged beneath
The slim-soled, treading women of his childhood dreams.
When he was in an obtuse rush, seen noxious and mean,
He was the trail and trace behind a dove aflutter: his queen…

And I, his long-time friend and confidant, sage confessor –
I was the cap of his oddest rage, his off-side, his creature's roar
Hung from the gibbet of his throat, dependent on the guiding core
Of his most private self: a tone, say, his wild music's source…

Utmost, then, was the unequal stance, an asymmetry
Trumpeted with all the keenness of brass, busy at its loudest ease.
Final, too, the stricken chord, the ill, the broken, the mauling noise –
The poet, the prosy passerby: two eyes, two ears, manning one body.

In The Beginning

I begin with this potted plant –
The bigger trees whose leaves dance
In the open-wide outside
Have different stories and
Different seers will tell them…

There's an empty chair standing before its
China blues and flowery reds, and
I don't know the names of the ghosts
Who come here to sit and inspect it, its rose
Colouring and rose scent.

I only know that it stands still, doesn't
Move or mummer in any way. And,
If I hang my watch on one of its leaves,
The time will be the same, I feel,
Hours later. It's captured here

As a spoken instance
Of an order of eternity
At a distance from us.
That's what I like about it:
That love's inside it.

Ligaments Between The Notes

After the Arab Spring, 2011

Strongholds and simple streams, my days are fitted with
A forking kind of sense.
                       Two beginnings.
                                     Where tangents kiss:
Forlorn petals, odd creatures, those whose norms are roaring loss…

I forget the date and time, I forget the wherewithal, my age, my
                                                   love.
I dream of freedom like a white digit dipped in, mixed with rum.

Rum-sweet, then, do you dawdle round the corner, welcome
As the fleets of thick fists which lift these
Fulsome agents' days
Against the plucked hull of despots?
Do you believe in something, anything, however tiny, tin-voiced,
                                           however small,
Arrived, risen?
So that stone may gain breath, inhale, and be sacrament?
So that the clambering might be ballet-sleek, ballet-tall?

So that the clamor of my prison-days without reason will
Shed the slim and all-deceptive skins: and the low, baroque sins
Of the snake and the snake's illusions,
Without end, without beginning?

Just so, words are arrows aimed at their quiet origins…
O God! Be plenty, alive in my quiver –
As I wander,
Beyond the slight mimesis of roads by rote,
Into another life of ligaments between the notes.

On Anger

For George Resek

It'd take an eon to sew the white without number,
The white between gaze and gazer,
The victorious beeline, the animal light,
The strong temptation of a jeweled heat.

My yesterday is close to my yesterday
And I remain alone, my own brawn and bruise.
I remain what my tongue cannot, will not say,
A lit-up figure, the clarity of a neck in a noose.

Everything I drink or eat now feeds this truth:
That I'm the sixth finger on a punching fist,
Gloriously short and fat and useless.
And broken as the bones smack and kiss.

The Hiding Place

Bleed this pointing finger,
Let it suffer to be scrawny and conquered,
As the picked-out objects of its beam and desire
Go to make a sum and sea of what she is, of lucky her
Ubiquitous in the dying blur
Of a dying sun,
                      a sinking sunken one
At the beginning of a star-decked future
And a night sweet as rum and dumb
When it comes to talking and totting figures
Of love, the giant numbers.

Wickedly, I surround myself with clouds
And callous words,
Hoping only in the above, like a leisured lord,
And dreaming a dream's absurd
And un-pick-able lock,
More jagged in its secrecy than feral rock:

As if a desert had nooks
And crannies,
                      as if the endless sand were
A hiding place like the heart.

Empty, Emptying

Just like that.
                    You are interred...
The mingling rocks of your body
                              speak
a harsh idiom on cue.
Your tongue is a dead leaf, desert yellow,
as you're bought and sold by
hollow-sounding shekels.

Nothing is true if slavery is true
and the once-hung stars return
to dead black matter.

O deep lions of my youth!
How in all the bother and blather
can one hoodwink a vacuum?

The Solitary, His Fate In Dream

The bird is heard by a whistling sound,
Uncontrolled, un-atoned
By the rapid intentions of brain or eye,
Its plummet-song a belfry torn

By storm and wind, its broken wings thin
As stencil paper, mere crust, mere bones
Of what was once so gladly worn
Like flapping goldleaf at its sides,

The way the whole of air was flown
Down to its most human concept:
Oxygen's swollen glory once,
And all the mice cleft by this

Arrow-bane of the sky's mischievous tides.
The bird weeps as it falls, knowing
A certain death.   Still aloof, though weeping,
A few seconds before pummelled to earth,

In its final puffed-out breath,
It whispers out the scratchy words
Once I hoped to outlast the poem
But now I know that's absurd